It's a Jungle Out There

It's a Jungle Out There

A Starry Safari from Angelemur Jolie to Oscar Wildebeest

Maureen Lipman

The Robson Press

First published in Great Britain in 2016 by
The Robson Press (an imprint of Biteback Publishing)
Westminster Tower
3 Albert Embankment
London SE1 7SP
Copyright © Maureen Lipman 2016

ISBN 978-1-78590-096-9

10 9 8 7 6 5 4 3 2 1

A CIP catalogue record for this book is available from the British Library.

Set in MrsEaves and Caslon by Adrian McLaughlin

Printed and bound in Great Britain by
CPI Group (UK) Ltd, Croydon CR0 4YY

MIX
Paper from
responsible sources
FSC® C020471

For my old swain Guido,
in lieu of all the hours I didn't spend on him.

My thanks to Olivia Beattie and all the team at The Robson Press, Stephen Johnson at Amber-Green, and Jeremy Robson, who went out on a limb for me.

Prologue

I need to doodle like a nine-month-old needs to teethe. It's not an option. I itch to sketch like Angelina itches to adopt. I can't physically take or make a phone call without a chewed biro and a scrap of paper, and the longer the conversation, the more alarming my doodle. Freud would have pinioned me to a couch; Lewis Carroll would have hired me. In my doodles, ears sprout foliage, trees have legs, pointy people in silhouette chase spotted pigs in top hats. Psychologically, it doesn't look good, but it actually keeps me sane. It may be chilling to the eye but it's chicken soup for the mind.

Often it starts with an eye. Then I add a socket and the idealised wide bone structure that I personally don't have. Then an elongated neck (of which I have rather too much), shampoo-advert hair – and just when things are looking vaguely *Vogue*-ish, I start to deconstruct. First comes a frown, then a few crow's feet; bags form beneath the lash-line, rings beneath the jawline, and before long I have my first completed crone. From there it's a short step to ominous crags, Gothic trees and, possibly, psychotherapy. Except this *is* my therapy. The cheap one, in which I phone a friend and discover not only that their woes are worse than mine, but that I've channelled Dali in the process.

My daughter has always doodled *Varks*. These are shy, hippo-like bipeds of her own creation, dressed in dungarees. They have biblical names, a perpetual hunger for chicken-and-leek pie, and enjoy queuing and being of service. Every desk diary I have, from 1980 onwards, is bordered and interlaced with the portly figure of Solomon Vark, waiting gravely for pie and instructions. At mealtimes I often had to play the role of Solomon Vark, whom I voiced as the love child of Dame Judi Dench and Neil Nunes.

My son's doodles have always been bolder, abstract and Manga; as befits the doodler whose boyhood reading was dominated by encyclopaedias, Asterix and Professor Branestawm. Probably his doodles are the best, though his natural diffidence prevents him from competing. 'No, *yours* are brilliant,' he'll murmur, waving away any compliment. 'Mine are rubbish.'

My late playwright husband Jack was a fine, self-taught, clay sculptor, but his patience wore thin at the compulsive doodling in our appointments diary. Every so often he'd come into the kitchen, sigh wearily at the gallery of crones, Varks and abstract Aztec profiles obliterating 'Monday', and stage a dramatic clean-up, followed by laboriously cutting the backs of old scripts into neat piles, drilling holes with a strange grey metal screwing device and threading them together with bootlaces. Hey presto – a family doodle pad!

No one used it. For the simple reason that a doodler's pad can't be mobile. Art must be created on a fixed surface, you see? With the hand that isn't holding the phone. And, in my family, none of our necks are short enough to comfortably rest the phone under our chins without dislocating our heads.

These days, at the front of my Tardis-like basement flat lives Nats, my PA and dog-whisperer. Nats is a real artist so she doesn't doodle on diaries. Instead, she has a tiny atelier in Portobello Road where she makes and sells her unique doodle clocks. Each one is individually cut from paper and intricately hand-drawn. When we met she was a film and television prop designer, temporarily living in her camper van. I offered her my daughter Amy's old room in the family house and ten years later, mercifully, she seems to be still around to change bulbs, understand boilers and doodle for a living.

My school friends were all real artists. Paddy was a bold, graphic painter, and the last I heard she was making artisan shoes in Suffolk. Marilyn became a specialist in miniature landscapes, settled in the Orkneys and wore out her eyes and knees crouching in fields with a magnifying glass. Me, I was the *actress*, I did Art at A-level but I knew my place. I still do. Nevertheless, I'm the unofficial cartoonist on every play I've been in. Every first-night card is a group portrait, replete with puns, and every script is covered in faces. I said *faces*, all right?

For years, that was my only form of art therapy. Then I joined an evening painting class at a multiplex studio in west London. A nightclub blared out house music in one space whilst, in the next, ferret-like daubers like myself were given a billy-can of water, acrylic paint, a huge canvas and carte blanche to go create. I'd get completely carried away. Suddenly, it would be two in the morning, I'd be splattered like a Jackson Pollock and the drunken revellers next door would come stumbling in to gape at the curious workings of my mind, laid bare in paint.

Nowadays my doodles happen largely on my iPad, on a remarkable app called Art Set. After all that splashing about with acrylics, charcoaling my extremities and collaging and decoupaging every surface in the flat, I've found Art Set's simple choices liberating. With my forefinger, I can paint, remove, crayon, remove, ink, remove, smudge, remove – without the whole work going brown from over-attention. Then, somehow, from under the layers, emerges the picture I wanted to paint. Revelation. And nothing to clear up! Some people use a special stylus on their iPad and I have tried and mislaid several but somehow my trusty finger is always at hand. You'll find me at my iPad at midnight and daybreak – or, as my late mother and much missed muse would have said, 'Every night that dawns.'

I paint portraits on there for friends' birthdays and special occasions, often managing, inadvertently, to offend them. It's easy to forget, as one joyfully experiments with colour and attempts, with love, to capture the essence of a person, how sensitive we all are about our looks. How we carry two versions of ourselves in our minds – the 'good version', which is how we like to see ourselves, and the 'bad', which draws on all our youthful insecurities. The reality is probably somewhere in between. My playwright daughter has a sideline painting families (from photographs) on Russian dolls. Even though the subjects provide the photographs themselves, she has to tread a fine line between accuracy and flattery.

Me, I draw from the pictures in my mind and my sense of the subject, and hope for the best.

Which brings me to this book. I've written nine previous books for Jeremy Robson at Robson Books. I began in 1985, back when jobbing actresses weren't known for compiling their life's anecdotes – especially when their life consisted of little more than leaving Hull for a London paved with feather boas and afros. Your best-selling autobiography was more in the line of David Niven's *The Moon's a Balloon* – all blazers and cravats, Hollywood Hills and the seduction of Princess Grace. Or *By Myself*, Lauren 'Betty' Bacall's cracking account of her life as movie star/siren, her affair with Sinatra, F. and marriage to hell-raiser Bogart, H. – which sold millions. But a myopic, happily married actress with one film (*Up the Junction*) two sitcoms (*Agony* and *All at Number Twenty*) and one episode of *Doctor in the House* behind her? It would surely be less book than pamphlet?

But Robson had faith and Lipman had the gift of the gob and a propensity to fall into surreal adventures on simply leaving the house. My first book, saucily titled *How Was It For You?*, became a UK number 1 seller thanks to frequent appearances on chat-show sofas and copious tours of Britain's bookshops with a biro. It was followed within a few years by *Something To Fall Back On*, *Thank you for Having Me*; *When's It Coming Out?*; *You Can Read Me Like a Book*; *Lip Reading*; *Past-It Notes* and two books of cartoon and verse: *You Got An Ology?* and *The Gibbon's in Decline, but the Horse is Stable*.

These books and my articles now serve me as a kind of portable memory, a reference library of where I was at any given time – and a way of recording those moments of hilarity or hubris that often take place when I'm on my own and beggar belief in retrospect. For instance, standing in tour group number 12 on the Galapagos Islands, waiting for a blue-footed booby to put in an appearance, when an elderly chap from group 13 scurries breathlessly across a pile of blue-footed booby poo to tap me on the shoulder and tell me that he didn't want to bother me when I was on holiday but he felt he must just tell me that when he was a boy in Hull he used to clean my Uncle Izzy's bike.

This book, by contrast, is a departure for me and for the Robson Press, and an act of faith on Jeremy's part. Because this is a collection of m'iPad paintings of famous people – crossed with animals. Yes, you read it right. And their names are tortuous puns on those of their animal doppelgangers, such as Meryl Sheep and Zebra Kerr. Sound like a best-seller? No, me neither.

It all began with a doodle of a steer in a dinner jacket with a long, mournful face. He reminded me of Oscar Wilde, so I gave him a green carnation and called him Oscar Wildebeest. Fast on his hooves followed Angelemur Jolie and Brad Pitt-Bull, Walrussell Brand and Labradoris Day and, relentlessly, seventy other finger paintings joined the pack.

So what should I call this eclectic collection? 'Paronomasia' is the official name for punning, but the combined faces of the Robson Press fell so low when I presented them with this that I had to buy them all a flat white and a biscotti to cheer them up.

Me: OK… How about *Dramatic Paws*?

Them: Yes!

Me: No. It reminds me of those hair salons called Curl Up and Dye.

Them: Oh.

Me: *Lionised by Lipman*?

Them: No lions in the book, though, are there?

Me: *WoMenagerie*?

Them: (searching desperately for a reason to resist this terrible pun) Half the animals you've drawn are men!

Me: *Pun Pals*?

Them: Are all these superstars your friends, then?

Me: *My-Pad*.

Them: Apple could sue.

Me: *Starry Safari?*

Them: Sounds like a Eurovision song.

Me: *One Drawn Every Minute.*

Them: Sounds like you spent no time working on it.

And so on. By the time I got to *The Origami of the Species* and *Beast Star Us*, I had to be put to bed with a hot milky drink and two drops of Rescue Remedy. I woke with a headful of pun-free titles, based on words I just *like*.

When Harry Otter Met Squirrelly Clinton... (It should be *When Harry Met Sally* but if I drew Sally Fieldmouse, would you know who I meant?)

A Dazzle of Zebras, a Firmament of Stars. (Sooo onomatopoetic but there's only one zebra in the book!)

I Did It with One Finger. I meant to imply that's what I use on the iPad, but the concerted response was that it sounds obscene.

And, as you can see whilst you sneak a look in the back of the Waterstones 'Humour' bin, in the end the simplest title won.

Let's talk about puns

Puns are the Marmite of word-play. I love a good one – but proper writers avoid them. Samuel Johnson nicknamed puns 'quibbles' and was affronted by Shakespeare's prolific use of them. It's true that I've witnessed actors bleeding through the ears to get a laugh out of punsters like Touchstone in *As You Like It*, or using tortuous Dudley accents to make *loins* sound exactly like *lines* so that the 'fatal *loins* of those two foes' in *Romeo and Juliet* has a dual meaning.

Often, those dual meanings are very much of their time. In *Twelfth Night*, Sir Andrew Aguecheek minces around agonising over a letter:

> What is 'pourquoi'? Do or not do? I would I had
> bestowed that time in the tongues, that I have in
> fencing, dancing, bear-baiting: Oh, had I but
> followed the arts!

'Then hadst thou had an excellent head of hair,' goads Sir Toby Belch.

'Why, would that have mended my hair?' Sir Andrew whines.

'Past question,' smirks his tormentor, 'for thou seest it will not curl by nature.'

To an Elizabethan audience, the word 'tongue' was pronounced *tong* and a tong was then, as now, a rudimentary flat-iron for curling hair. Maybe it won't have them rolling in the aisles in 2016 but, back then, it was a pleasing gag. '*All the world's a stage*' wrote the maestro, who had called his theatre The Globe. It is a philosophy and a pun in one.

The art of punning goes back to the Sumerian cuneiform, which sounds like an underwired bra, but here's what I was told by the fantastically white-bearded, cuneiform and hieroglyphics supremo at the British Museum, Irving Finkel:

'An Akaadian scribe got bored with chronicling endless daily records of battles won. He was engaged in carving into clay wedges the defeat of the city of Lulubum when he decided to turn it into a private joke. He punned from the Sumarian *Lu lu* into the Babylonian I II I II.

'Are you with me?' He asked.

'Er...' I replied.

Reassured, he continued:

'In Sumerian, *he* is part of the verbal system which, placed before a verbal root, means *may it be that*. In Akkadian, the corresponding grammatical particle with the same meaning is *lu*. Therefore the scribe has written he-he instead of *lu lu*. "*He he*, indeed." The scribe must have rubbed his hands in glee producing a conundrum for his fellow clerks.

'"No, missus! Listen – it's the way I carve it!"'

When I asked my classically inclined son for an appropriate pun, he said, 'Oooh, I love a man in cuneiform,' and reminded me of the dramatic telegram, allegedly from General Napier to the Foreign Office after the recapture of the Indian city of Sindh: 'Peccavi', it said. In Latin: 'We have sinned.'

From Restoration comedy to vaudeville and music hall, all the way to Donald McGill's seaside postcards, the pun and the double entendre have thrived. 'I have it from one, who has it from one, who has it from the Prince of Wales.' Was that gossip, wondered Congreve's audience, or venereal disease? 'A little bit of what you fancy does you good,' chirped Marie Lloyd with a sweetly ambiguous innocence, and 'Keep your hand on your ha'penny, cover it well with your palm,' trilled Kitty McShane – referring to a currency, no doubt, but not the one that bought you a pint of porter.

In Patrick O'Brian's *Master and Commander*, Jack draws Stephen's attention to a pair of weevils on a plate of crumbs.

'Which would you choose?'

'There is not a scrap of difference. *Arcades ambo*. They are the same species of *curculio*, and there is nothing to choose between them.'

'But suppose you had to choose?'

'Then I should choose the right-hand weevil; it has a perceptible advantage in both length and breadth.'

'There I have you,' cried Jack. 'You are completely dished. Don't you know that in the navy you must always choose the lesser of two weevils?'

And better still for the punsters amongst us, it's said that when the lyricist Frank Loesser (*Guys and Dolls*) followed his waspish wife into a party, some wag was heard to murmur, 'Here comes the evil of two Loessers.'

Of course, all credit for the definitive 'wish I'd said that' pun goes to the great Dorothy Parker, doyenne of the literary wits who gathered at the Algonquin Hotel. Challenged in a game to use the word 'horticulture' in a sentence, she came up with the sublime: 'You can lead a whore to culture but you cannot make her think.'

My trivial brain is forever silently punning. Simply spreading something on my morning toast makes me long to be a copywriter: 'I'm pink, therefore I'm jam.' Originally, the heroine of 'my' BT adverts was called Doris. At my audition I suggested they name her Beattie, and that's maybe why I got the part. But the nearest I ever got to my own personal Algonquin came when I was filming in a garden with the actor Michael Jayston. He marvelled at the size and beauty of the peonies before us: 'I wish I could grow peonies like that in my garden.' Without skipping a beat, I accused him of peonies envy.

Some years back, I created a calendar to raise money for Myeloma UK, after this insidious blood cancer took away my husband Jack and devastated our family. For each of the twelve months I drew one of the pun-inspired characters I created as a schoolgirl to amuse my friends. There was Sheila Blige and Edna Clouds … Francesca U. Knighted … Jacqueline Hyde, Adelaide Reaction. As it was in the beginning…

And so, for this book, I chose my celebrated subjects based on their punnability more than their resemblance to animals. Famous names like Virginia Woolf or Tiger Woods seem ripe for anthropomorphism, but where's the pun in that? Cat Stevens, Bear Grylls, Rudyard Kipper-ling, Angela Eagle and Cardinal Ratzinger sprang to mind but not to finger, whilst Nicola Sturgeon and Alex Salmond leave the paronomasiac on dry land. I *was* somewhat drawn to draw Ryan Gosling, and tempted by Rhino Neal, George St Bernard Shaw and Mahatma Gander – but a girl has to stop somewhere and, frankly, I could do with a good night's kip. No, less is Maureen – pun intended.

Throughout the book I have added a few favourite animal jokes to expand on my theme. With political correctness as rife as it now is, there are tight restrictions on humour. We can't satirise the Irish community, or the black, or the Asian, or the Polish; we can't poke fun at the wife or the mother-in-law either. And in some ways this is how it should be. And yet there is no humour from time immemorial without someone superior looking down on an inferior. I shudder to think of some of the jokes I've heard and told in my life, quite innocent of the fact that they reinforced appalling stereotypes. Lord, though, they were funny.

These days, it is only appropriate *for me* to tell Jewish jokes, blonde jokes, age jokes, lawyer jokes, golf jokes and animal jokes – and, let's face it, even these will probably soon be an endangered species. Aren't we all? I have just, to my disbelief, turned seventy – and yet I seem to be no older, no wiser and permanently up for a laugh. I hope you are too.

Maureen Lipman

July 2016

A percentage of the sales of this book go to Myeloma UK.

Elvers Presley

Nigel Farog

Angelemur Jolie

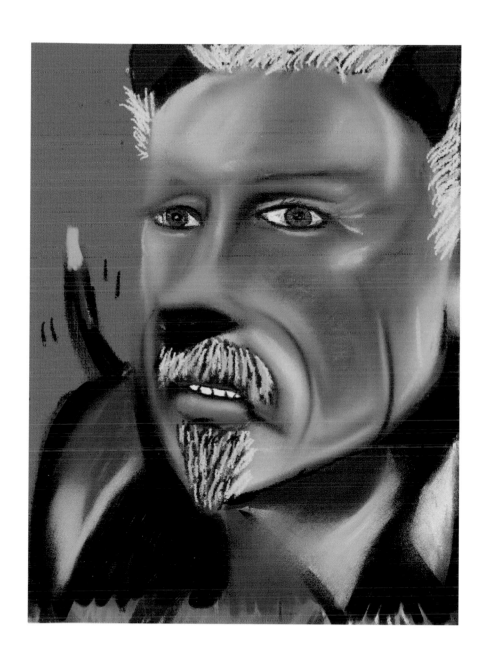

Brad Pitt-Bull

Placido Flamingo

Luciano Pandarotti

David Cormorant

Jeremy Macawbyn

Ant & Duck

A duck checks into a small hotel with his potential duck mistress. Once in the room, she asks him if he has a condom. He blanches and says he hadn't thought about it.

'Well, think about it now,' she snaps. 'I'm not just any old duck, you know. Have you never heard of safe sex?'

'Err ... how do I?'

'Oh, just ring down to room service and ask them to send one up. Honestly!' She goes into the shower.

The duck calls room service and says:

'It's err ... Mr Duck in Room 75. Err ... could I possibly have a ... err, a ... cup of tea for two and a ... c-c-clotted cream scone and ... err ... a condom? Thank you.'

He puts down the phone and waits. There is a knock at the door and the waiter comes in with a tray.

'Here you are, sir, two teas, one scone and a condom. Shall I put it on your bill?'

'What do you think I am, a pervert?'

Yeti Davis

Joan Crowford

Angela Meerkat

General Charles De Gull

Slow Loris Johnson

Forrest Trump

Barry Manatee

Ellafantz Gerald

The story goes that Bill Clinton flew in from the Deep South on Air Force One and was greeted by a young intern, who was astounded to see that the President had a small piglet under each arm.

'I got them for Hillary and Chelsea,' smiles Clinton.

Relieved, the intern grinned from ear to ear and said:

'Good swap, sir, good swap!'

polar bear cub is out on the ice. He asks his mum:

'Mum, have I got a bit of grizzly bear in me?'

Mum says fondly: 'No, darling, you're a polar bear.'

'Mum,' he continues, 'have I got a bit of panda in me, then?'

'No, you don't, you are a polar bear!'

'But Mum, have I just got a bit of brown bear in me?'

'Darling, you are a polar bear through and through. Why do you keep asking me these questions?'

''Cos I'm bloody freezing.'

Vladimir Puffin

Moth Teresa

Wayne Kangarooney

Giraffa Nadal

Barack Obllama

Squirrelly Clinton

William Snakespeare

Wolfgang Armadillo Mozart

Ewe Jackman

Meryl Sheep

Dame Jedi Dench

Nessie Redgrave

Benedict Humperback

Tuna Stubbs

After Noah had completed his historic voyage, he continued living into his eighth century. One day he heard the voice of the Lord asking him once more to build an ark.

'Oh, Lord, please not again – the same ark?'

No, Noah, this time I desire you to build an ark of twenty storeys.'

'Twenty storeys! My Lord – I am an old man—'

'It shall be so!' thundered the Lord.

'And will you require the same pairs of animals of every species, my Lord?' mumbles Noah.

'No, my son,' says the Lord. 'Fish.'

Noah gasps:

'Every species of fish?'

'No, no, Noah,' sighs the Lord. 'Just carp.'

Noah scratches his ancient pate:

'You want me to build an ark on twenty levels and fill every level with carp?'

'It shall be so.'

'Forgive me, my Lord, but might I ask what is the reason for this request? Has man once again defied your laws? Has the Devil infiltrated the soul of mankind? Why?'

'Dunno really,' admits the Lord, 'I just fancy seeing a multi-storey carp ark.'

woman took her dog to the vet because of his hearing loss. The vet told her the dog's ears were blocked by hair growth and gave her an ointment to apply. On doing so, the woman realised it was the same hair remover she used herself but at nine times the price. The dog's hearing recovered but, inevitably, the hair regrew, so the next time she went straight to the pharmacy and asked for her own, cheap, hair remover. The pharmacist wrapped it up and warned:

'If this cream is for underarm growth, don't use a deodorant for a few days.'

'No, it isn't for under my arms,' replied the woman.

'Well, if it's for your legs, use a moisturiser for a few days.'

'No ... it's not for my legs,' she hedges.

Intrigued, the chemist asks:

'May I ask what you're using the cream for exactly?'

'It's for my schnauzer.'

'OK,' says the pharmacist, 'then don't ride your bike for a week.'

Dingo Starr

Bruce Springbok

Harry Otter

Moggy Smith

Manxy

Pigasso

Maredonna & Lady Gee-Gee

Orson Wheels

A horse walks into a bar and orders champagne, brandy and a tequila. The barman delivers them, but the horse shakes his head ruefully and says:

'It's terrible. I shouldn't really be drinking these. Not with what I've got.'

'Why?' says the barman. 'What have you got?'

'20p and a carrot.'

A white horse goes into a bar. The barman says:

'We've got a whisky named after you.'

The horse looks amazed. 'What?' he says, 'Eric?'

Leonaardvark DiCaprio

Jake Gorillenhaal

Gnatalie Klein

Camel Parker Bowles

Two old ladies are smoking outside their care home. When it starts to rain, Bessie removes a plastic sheath from her pocket, cuts off the end and continues smoking a dry cigarette. Millie, her friend, asks what the little plastic sheath is?

'It's a condom,' says Bessie. 'You should buy one at the pharmacy.'

Millie goes there right away and asks for a condom. 'What size?' asks the chemist.

'Size? Erm… I don't know…'

'Well, do you want small, medium or large?'

Millie thinks for a moment and says:

'I just want one big enough to cover a Camel.'

A shark captures a small squid, who protests wildly:

'Don't eat me, don't eat me! I've been really ill. I've had 'flu and tonsillitis and a bilious attack — you won't like the taste of me!'

The shark spits out the squid but keeps hold of it and swims down to the bottom of the ocean. He knocks on a door and a killer whale comes out. 'What do you want?' says the whale.

The shark grins:

'I've brought you the sick squid I owe you.'

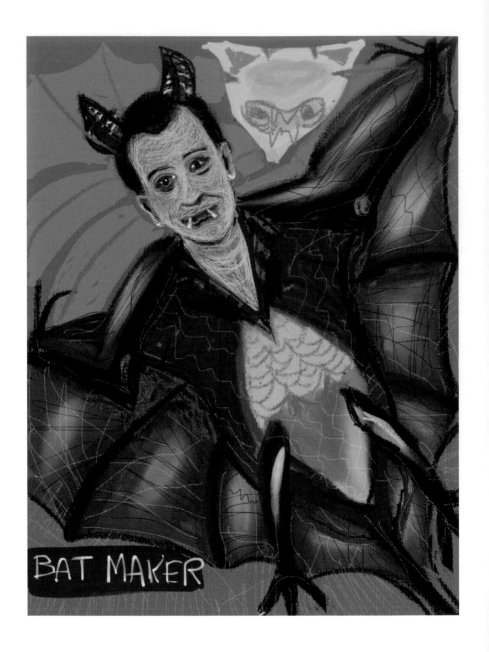

Batt Maker

Oryx Jones

Greyhound Norton

Hyena Sharples

Luseal Ball

Hippo Marx

Puma Thurman

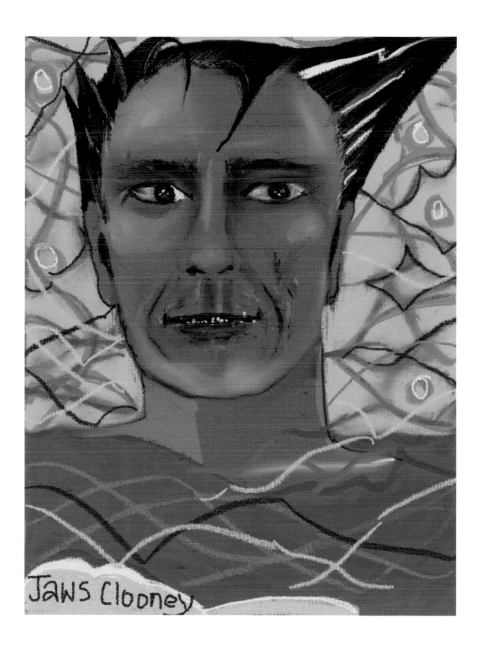

Jaws Clooney

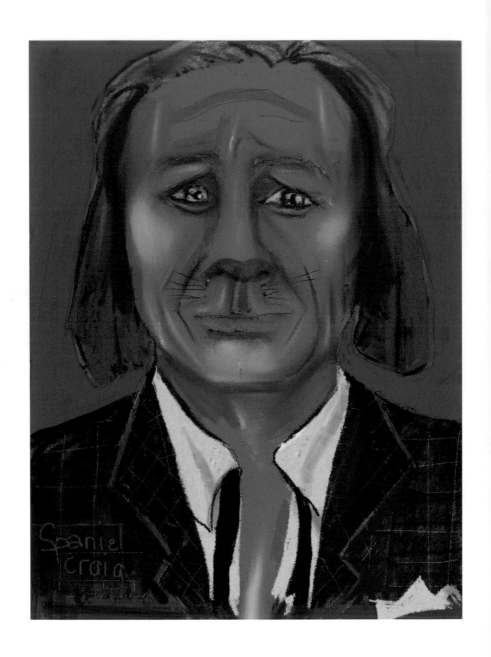

Spaniel Craig

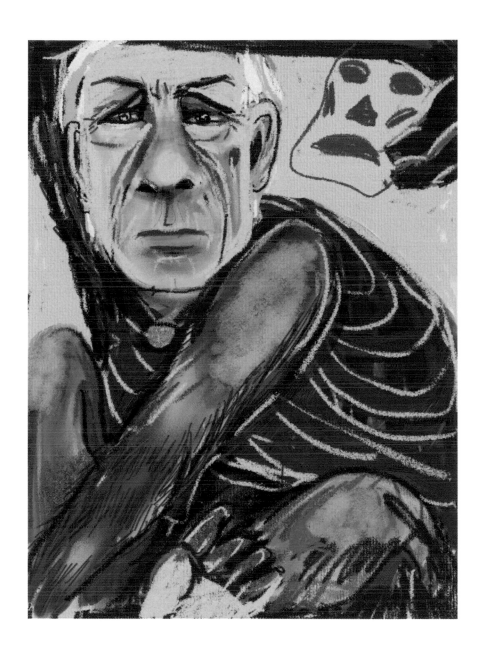

Simian McKellen

Terry, a *Sun* reader, took two stuffed dogs to the *Antiques Roadshow.*

'Oooh!' said the presenter. 'This is a very rare set, produced by the celebrated Johns Brothers, who operated in London at the turn of the century. Do you have any idea what they would fetch if they were in good condition?'

Terry scratched his head for a moment, then replied, 'Sticks.'

A grizzly goes into a pub and says to the barman:

'I want a large gin and...'

He stops, the barman waits, the bear thinks for a while and finally says:

'... and tonic, please.'

The barman gives him the drink and says:

'Sorry, sir, but why the big pause?'

The bear holds up his hands:

'I'm a feckin' bear, aren't I?'

Andy Warthog

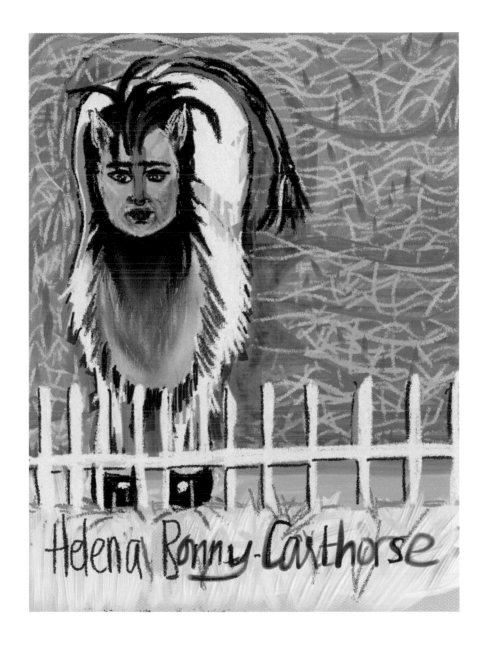

Helena Bonny-Carthorse

Sir Ian Slotham

Mick Jaguar

Sir Tim Mice & Andrew Pied Warbler

Badgers & Hammerhead

Labradoris Day

Airdele

Sir Ian Lemming

Dame Vera Lynx

Jackal Nicholson

Sean Pennguin

Sir Alfred Spatchcock

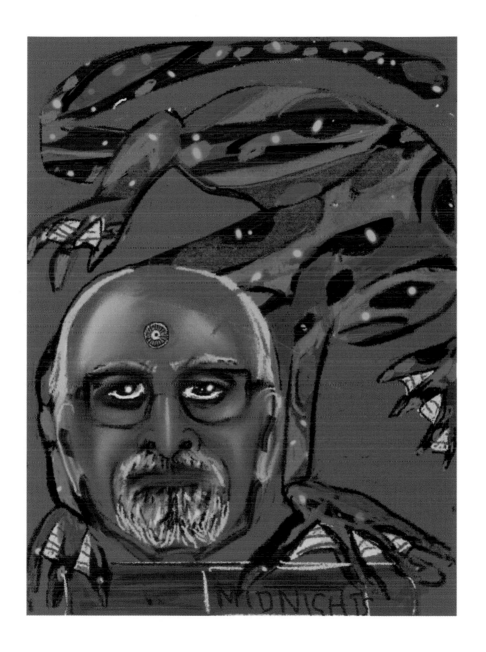

Salamander Rushdie

Oscar Wildebeest

Christopher Buggins

Grizzly Joseph

Catherine Chimpanzeeta-Jones

An Anglican vicar, a Catholic priest and a Jewish rabbi have a bet as to which of them could convert a bear. The Anglican sees the bear by a forest, pushes him down onto his knees and, before he can recover, he baptises him. The Catholic sees the bear by the river and pushes him in and, while he is swimming back, he baptises him.

The pair hear that the rabbi is in hospital. They visit him. He is in traction from head to foot with eighty breakages to his body.

'What happened?' ask the pair in horror.

The rabbi responds softly through his splinted jaw:

'I suppose, in retrospect, I shouldn't have started with the circumcision.'

A man sees his friend walking down Bayswater Road with a chimp on each arm. He says:

'What are you doing with those chimps?'

The man looks rueful: 'Oh, a friend of mine left them with me. He's gone abroad. No idea what to do with them.'

'Well, I should take them to a zoo if I were you.'

'Yeah, you're probably right.'

A week later he sees the man again, walking down Shaftesbury Avenue with a chimp on each arm.

'I thought you were going to take them to a zoo,' he says.

'I did,' replies his friend. 'They loved it, so today I'm taking them to a matinee.'

Al Pacacino

John Travoleta

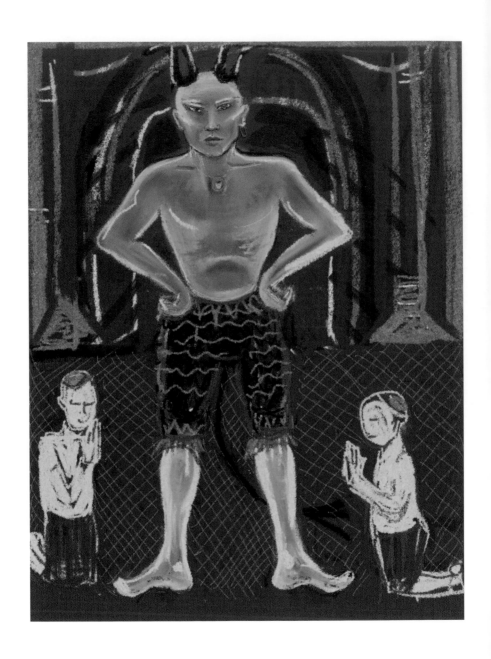

Mul Brynner

Zebra Kerr

Walrussell Brand

Johnny Deppard

Rupert Leveret